DOGS AS I SEE THEM

DOGS AS I SEE THEM

by

LUCY DAWSON

Mac

With 22 Illustrations in Color

GROSSET & DUNLAP

Publishers　　　　NEW YORK

Printed in the United States of America

DOGS AS I SEE THEM

Lucy Dawson's friendly, sympathetic portraits of dogs so delighted readers of numerous English and American periodicals that they finally were gathered together to make a book.

With her sketches are her own amusing notes about the conduct of the dogs while they posed. These charming little reminiscences interpret the character and mood of each and make us friends at once with every one in this gallery of engaging portraits.

The artist herself says that it is because dogs feel and portray to the full the emotions of love, hate, fear, trust, humor that she loves them, both as friends and as models for her pictures.

In her own words: "An old dog dreaming before the fire, a dog in the perfection of its mature strength romping with a friend, either canine or human, a puppy sitting thinking of the puzzling wonderments of life—they make the dog-lover in me thrill with happiness and the artist in me itch for my drawing materials."

BINKIE

Very, very young, and quite unaccustomed to sitting on a table. Moreover, the table was slippery and only the kind attention of his owner kept him on it at all. But Binkie was fascinated with my scratchings on paper and couldn't think why he was such an object of interest.

Binkie

JOAN

A very shy little cairn, friend and companion of Ian, who is winner of many prizes. The lucky little dogs spend glorious holidays in Cornwall each year.

BOB

My constant companion for five years——a little stray who was found exhausted under a hedge when about 18 months old. He always lay on the couch in my studio, "sleeping" with one eye open to see what I was up to and never forgetting to tell me when it was lunch-time.

I always remember, when spending a holiday at my little country cottage one summer, how Bob buried bones in the cornfield the day he arrived. On the day we returned poor Bob couldn't find his precious bones because the corn had been cut in the meantime so that he lost his bearings! We nearly lost our homeward 'bus as well. Dear old Bob!

My Tailwagger

Luc Dawson

Before the trimming

— and after

That hot day!

NANKI POO

I journeyed from London to a lovely bit of country in Northamptonshire in order to draw him, but that, of course, didn't impress Nanki Poo, who is accustomed to such attentions and only condescended to lie the right way up just long enough for me to make the colored sketch. I think you can judge from the other sketches how he behaved for the rest of the time. Anyhow, I suppose he must be excused for being rather "upsidedownish," as he is very beautiful.

JANE

Jane's sole care is the baby son of her master and mistress. She keeps such a careful guard over him that I had the impression she thought I was not to be trusted. Jane lives a family life and, although a sporting dog, I don't think she worries much about it. But never mind, she is very healthy and happy and unspoiled—which is the main thing.

Jane

OONAGH

A wire-haired dachshund of some distinction who welcomes me most kindly. I should really have drawn her in a begging position as she seems to be able to sit up indefinitely, which always puzzles me when I look at her very long back.

Lucy Dawson

Wire haired Dachshund

"Odnach"

CREENAGH

Often I visit a kennel of little "Scotties," and their boisterous greeting never fails to take me out of myself when in low spirits. Almost they persuade me that I am their greatest friend—but biscuits can explain a lot. Janet and Creenagh are old friends of mine, and the industry and perseverance of their race are illustrated by the way in which they will beg for hours on end—to the very last biscuit. As professional models they demand a very high rate of biscuits per hour.

Janet begging

Fireside meditation

Janet

My neighbours — seen from my window

DEENA

Deena, whose home is in London, prefers to live in Cornwall. She is celebrated for her smile which she always effects when told she is naughty, so that her owners find it difficult to scold her. Certainly a broad smile on a sealyham is most disarming. In London she dislikes walking (on account of the pavements—I believe sealyhams' feet are often very tender), but in Cornwall she spends her time out of doors—hunting if given a chance.

Deena doesn't care.

ALBERT

Albert is Deena's son, with all her characteristics—and just as lovable. We met when he was only a few weeks old at his home near the Albert Bridge—hence his name. He soon got to know (perhaps Deena told him) that if he kept changing his position whilst being a model he would be given a piece of biscuit to gain his attention. As his owner doesn't approve of such manner of feeding, our sittings often came to naught. Moreover, Albert was temperamental and being a model didn't always appeal to him.

The interval.

ALBERT.

Albert   mac.

JOAN AND MINNIE

I thought Joan (the bulldog) would look very nice sitting up, but on being left to ourselves Joan decided otherwise and got under a chair for shelter. Every time I moved the chair Joan followed, so in desperation I left her there. Somehow I managed to get what you see on the opposite page. Minnie ignored me. They only sprang into life when their mistress returned.

BORIS

Several times I had watched Boris walking with his mistress, and one day I took my courage in both hands and asked permission to draw him. Here he is, and a very noble fellow I found him. Wanda, whom you see in black-and-white, is strangely musical, so her mistress kindly played the piano during the sitting and chose some favorite music. Wanda likes classical music and dislikes anything of a jazzy nature. She will lie quietly for hours listening to music that she enjoys.

PATCH

This young woman—pretty and mild-eyed—was my visitor in the country for five weeks last spring. Generally she is very well behaved, so three days' absence rabbit-hunting was more than we expected and decidedly disconcerting. A favorite trick of hers is to stalk some unwary dog and suddenly and noiselessly pounce upon him —just as a joke. All dogs are perfect little gentlemen and take it very well, but it wasn't quite such a joke the day she selected one of her own sex!

As a companion and mother Patch has few equals, and we must make some allowances for our friends.

The next day -
or sleeping it "Up"

"Patch"
after the 3 days
Rabbit hunt

GEORGE

A great little dog of no small importance in his home. He conscientiously guards his mistress and everything belonging to her—he would give his little life if necessary.

"Tea Time"

RED PRINCE OF WU SUNG

Now here is a super show-dog. I had to have the help of the owner, well known as a chow breeder, to be sure that I got his points right. He has won many prizes at the best shows and so has his daughter Lalli. They live in a kennel in company with the most charming chows of all ages. Red Prince and Lalli are perfectly sweet in disposition, and delightful companions.

"Bruce of WU-SUNG"

Red Prince of
Winsong

BERBAY'S LAD AND THE
SIAMESE CAT

A cat-and-dog life—but not on traditional lines. A boisterous fellow, Laddie, from whom I get a most enthusiastic greeting—but his cat friend politely ignores me. I am told she knows everything that is said to her for "Siamese cats are different" and more intelligent than the ordinary cat. That means they must know a lot because our own cats are certainly not stupid.

"Bertram's Lad"

"Laddie"

"Nong Tai"

BILLY

Of aristocratic breed, Billy was quite young when the sketch was made—very beautiful by nature and beautiful to look at. Most intelligent and definitely a "one-man dog." He suffers fools gladly but he's very difficult to get to know.

"BILLY"

Golden Retriever

MIKE

Now Mike is no show dog, but he is very proud of the fact that he is directly descended from King Edward VII.'s dog Caesar. Full of character and extremely intelligent, I've drawn him almost since he was born, and I hope he has a long, happy life in front of him.

Jack. Cairn & Fox-terrier

Mike

Mike

CAESAR

One of the few dogs who are content to come along to the studio without his owner. He spends the day with me quite happily although we are only slightly acquainted. A jolly little companion. I covet so many of these models, but my own dog sees to it that no others share his home. In fact he rather bullies me.

MALICK AND WOODIE

An occasional biscuit kept the attention of this happy pair. When weary of tit-bits they went to sleep, which suited me very well. When awake they can be quite lively, as any one who knows this breed will appreciate.

TRIG

Trig is a very affectionate soul and nearly eats me up with pleasure when I go and see him. Always full of fun, and a good, if not easy, subject to sketch. He did find the chair slippery, but he knew he must not get down. You can see that look in his expression.

Lakeland Terrier

Tea time

PATRICK

Patrick lived to a ripe old age. He had a lovely home at Thames Ditton and I very much regret I was unable to get more sketches of him before he died. He was a wonderful model, and his constant companion was a handsome Dalmatian.

At Random

"Lucky Star" 1930

Still more "at Random"

Algerian Sheep dog

ALBERT.